RUMI's QUOTES

THAT WILL EXPAND YOUR MIND

This book is adapted from the Rumi's life.

BURHAN UNVER

Who was Rumi?

Maulana Jalaluddin Rumi was a 13th century Persian poet, an Islamic dervish and a Sufi mystic. He is regarded as one of the greatest spiritual masters and poetical intellects. Born in 1207 AD, he belonged to a family of learned theologians. He made use of everyday life's circumstances to describe the spiritual world. Rumi's poems have acquired immense popularity, especially among the Persian speakers of Afghanistan, Iran and Tajikistan. Numerous poems written by the great poet have been translated to different languages.

Rumi's father was Bahā ud-Dīn Walad, a scholar, legal adviser and a spiritualist from Balkh, who was additionally referred to by the adherents of Rumi as Sultan al-Ulama or "Sultan of the Scholars".The most imperative impacts upon Rumi, other than his father, were the Persian artists Attar and Sanai. Rumi communicates his appreciation: "Attar was the spirit, Sanai his eyes twain, And in time thereafter, Came we in their train"

He further appreciates the two in another sonnet: "Attar has traversed the seven cities of Love, We are still at the turn of one street".

Rumi's works are written mostly in Persian, but occasionally he also used Turkish, Arabic, and Greek in his verse. His Mathnawī, composed in Konya, is considered one of the greatest poems of the Persian language.

He is regarded as one of the most popular and accomplished poets of all times, and he has been best selling poet in the United States of America. Rumi's work is so relevant to the modern day world that it trends on internet even to this date.

Here are some Rumi Quotes.

"A craftsman pulled a reed from the ree bed, cut holes in it, and called it a human being. Since then, it's been wailing a tender agony of parting, never mentioning the skill that gave it life as a flute"

"A wealth you cannot imagine flows through you. Do not consider what strangers say. Be secluded in your secret heart-house, that bowl of silence."

"Be quiet now and wait. It may be that the ocean one, the one we desire so to move into and become, desires us out here on land a little longer, going our sundry roads to the shore.
"Dear soul, don't set a high value on someone before they deserve it; You either lose them or ruin yourself…!"

"Die! Die! Die in this love! If you die in this love, Your soul will be renewed. Die! Die! Don't fear the death of that which is known If you die to the temporal, You will become timeless."

"Do not seek water, get thirst."

"Everything you possess of skill, and wealth, and handicraft, wasn't it first merely a thought and a quest?"

"For the thirst to possess your love, is worth my blood a hundred times."

"I will soothe you and heal you, I will bring you roses. I too have been covered with thorns."

"I know you're tired but come, this is the way. "For without you, I swear, the town Has become like a prison to me. Distraction and the mountain And the desert, all I desire."

"If I could repeat it, people passing by would be enlightened and go free."

"If there were no way into God, I would not have lain in the grave of this body so long."

"Love calls – everywhere and always. We're sky bound. Are you coming?"

"Like a sculptor, if necessary, carve a friend out of stone. Realize that your inner sight is blind and try to see a treasure in everyone."

"Love isn't the work of the tender and the gentle; Love is the work of wrestlers. The one who becomes a servant of lovers is really a fortunate sovereign. Don't ask anyone about Love; ask Love about Love . Love is a cloud that scatters pearls."

"Lovers find secret places inside this violent world where they make transactions with beauty."

Wherever you are, and whatever you do, be in love...

We carry inside us the wonders we seek outside us.

The moment you accept what troubles you've been given, the door will open.

Your heart knows the way. Run in that direction.

These pains you feel are messengers. Listen to them.

Stop acting so small. You are the universe in ecstatic motion.

Love is the bridge between you and everything.

Only from the heart can you touch the sky.

Keep silent, because the world of silence is a vast fullness.

The desire to know your own soul will end all other desires.

When will you begin that long journey into yourself?

Let silence take you to the core of life.

You are not a drop in the ocean. You are the entire
ocean, in a drop.

Whatever lifts the corners of your mouth, trust that.

My soul is from elsewhere, I'm sure of that, and I
intend to end up there.

Yesterday I was clever, so I wanted to change the world. Today I am wise, so I am changing myself.

There is a candle in your heart, ready to be kindled. There is a void in your soul, ready to be filled. You feel it, don't you?

Be like a tree and let the dead leaves drop.

I have been a seeker and I still am, but I stopped asking the books and the stars. I started listening to the teaching of my Soul.

It's your road and yours alone. Others may walk it
with you, but no one can walk it for you.
Let silence be the art you practice.

In the blackest of your moments, wait with no fear.

By God, when you see your beauty you will be the
idol of yourself.

Maybe you are searching among the branches, for
what only appears in the roots.

I want to sing like the birds sing, not worrying about who hears or what they think.

What matters is how quickly you do what your soul directs.

The whole universe is contained within a single human being – you.

The spirit is so near that you can't see it! But reach for it… don't be a jar, full of water, whose rim is always dry. Don't be the rider who gallops all night and never sees the horse that is beneath him.

Take someone who doesn't keep score, who's not looking to be richer, or afraid of losing, who has not the slightest interest even in his own personality: he's free.

When the world pushes you to your knees, you're in the perfect position to pray.

Be full of sorrow, that you may become hill of joy; weep, that you may break into laughter.

There is a voice that doesn't use words, listen.

In silence there is eloquence. Stop weaving and see how the pattern improves.

I am not this hair, I am not this skin, I am the soul that lives within.

Close your eyes, fall in love, stay there. (This is one of my favorite quote. Leave a reply here and let me know what's yours!)

What you seek is seeking you.

Let the beauty we love be what we do.

There are hundreds of ways to kneel and kiss the ground.

Run from what's comfortable. Forget safety. Live where you fear to live. Destroy your reputation. Be notorious. I have tried prudent planning long enough. From now on I'll be mad.

Your task is not to seek for love, but merely to seek and find all the barriers within yourself that you have built against it.

Sell your cleverness and buy bewilderment. Cleverness is mere opinion. Bewilderment brings intuitive knowledge.

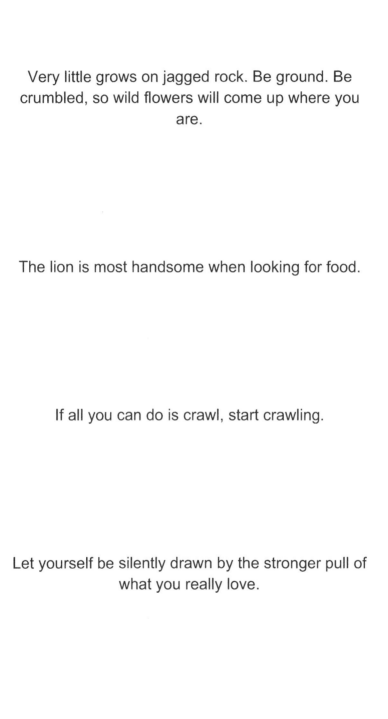

Very little grows on jagged rock. Be ground. Be crumbled, so wild flowers will come up where you are.

The lion is most handsome when looking for food.

If all you can do is crawl, start crawling.

Let yourself be silently drawn by the stronger pull of what you really love.

Raise your words, not voice. It is rain that grows flowers, not thunder.

When you do things from your soul, you feel a river moving in you, a joy.

Life is balance of holding on and letting go.

SHORT RUMI QUOTES

Patience is the key to joy.

If light is in your heart, you will find your way home.

Set your life on fire. Seek those who fan your flames.

Dance until you shatter yourself.

Be empty of worrying. Think of who created thought.

As you start to walk on the way, the way appears.

Become the sky. Take an axe to the prison wall. Escape.

Let yourself become living poetry.
Be drunk with love, for love is all that exists.

Be soulful. Be kind. Be in love.

Be an empty page, untouched by words.

I know you're tired but come, this is the way.

The wealth within you, your essence, is your kingdom.

To praise the sun is to praise your own eyes.

What hurts you, blesses you. Darkness is your candle.

Respond to every call that excites your spirit.

Wherever you stand, be the soul of that place.

You were born with wings. Why prefer to crawl through life?

Half-heartedness doesn't reach into majesty.

Look at the moon in the sky, not the one in the lake.

What is planted in each person's soul will sprout.

The source of now is here.

Grace comes to forgive and then forgive again.

INSPIRATIONAL RUMI QUOTES

You are not meant for crawling, so don't. You have wings. Learn to use them and fly.

Anyone who genuinely and consistently with both hands looks for something, will find it.

In each moment the fire rages, it will burn away a hundred veils. And carry you a thousand steps toward your goal.

There is a life-force within your soul, seek that life. There is a gem in the mountain of your body, seek that mine. O traveller, if you are in search of that, don't look outside, look inside yourself and seek that.

With every breath, I plant the seeds of devotion, I am a farmer of the heart.

Everyone has been made for some particular work, and the desire for that work has been put in every heart.

Achieve some perfection yourself, so that you may not fall into sorrow by seeing the perfection in others.

Don't be satisfied with stories, how things have gone with others. Unfold your own myth.

Whether one moves slowly or with speed, the one who is a seeker will be a finder.

Be a lamp, or a lifeboat, or a ladder. Help someone's soul heal. Walk out of your house like a shepherd.

Let us carve gems out of our stony hearts and let them light our path to love.

Start a huge, foolish project, like Noah… it makes absolutely no difference what people think of you.

Seek the wisdom that will untie your knot. Seek the path that demands your whole being
Whoever has heart's doors wide open, could see the sun itself in every atom.

The message behind the words is the voice of the heart.

You are not one you are a thousand. Just light your lantern.

DEEP AND EMOTIONAL RUMI QUOTES

If you are irritated by every rub, how will your mirror be polished?

I have neither a soul nor a body, for I come from the very Soul of all souls.

When someone beats a rug, the blows are not against the rug, but against the dust in it.

Concentrate on the Essence, concentrate on the light.

Why do you stay in prison when the door is so wide open?

Beyond the rightness or wrongness of things there is a field, I'll meet you there.

Something opens our wings. Something makes boredom and hurt disappear. Someone fills the cup in front of us: We taste only sacredness.

Every need brings what's needed. Pain bears its cure like a child. Having nothing produces provisions. Ask a difficult question, and the marvelous answer appears.

The soul has been given its own ears to hear things mind does not understand.

Discard yourself and thereby regain yourself.
Spread the trap of humility and ensnare love.

All that you think is rain is not. Behind the veil angels sometimes weep.

Inside any deep asking is the answering.

Wisdom tells us we are not worthy; love tells us we are. My life flows between the two.

My words are like a ship, and the sea is their meaning. Come to me and I will take you to the depths of spirit. I will meet you there.

Ignore those that make you fearful and sad, that degrade you back towards disease and death.

The time has come to turn your heart into a temple of fire.

Open your hands if you want to be held.

Be melting snow. Wash yourself of yourself.

The soul is here for its own joy.

Seek the sound that never ceases. Seek the sun that never sets.

WISE RUMI QUOTES (WORDS OF WISDOM)

Conventional opinion is the ruin of our souls.

Whatever purifies you is the right path, I will not try to define it.

Let go of your mind and then be mindful. Close your ears and listen.

The world is a mountain, in which your words are echoed back to you.

Laugh as much as you breathe. Love as long as you live.

All your anxiety is because of your desire for harmony. Seek disharmony, then you will gain peace.

Anything which is more than our necessity is poison. It may be power, wealth, hunger, ego, greed, laziness, love, ambition, hate or anything.

Poetry can be dangerous, especially beautiful poetry, because it gives the illusion of having had the experience without actually going through it.

In their seeking, wisdom and madness are one and the same. On the path of love, friend and stranger are one and the same.

Clean out your ears, don't listen for what you already know.

O, happy the soul that saw its own faults.

When you lose all sense of self, the bonds of a thousand chains will vanish.

Peaceful is the one who's not concerned with having more or less. Unbound by name and fame, he is free from sorrow from the world and mostly from himself.

Two there are who are never satisfied – the lover of the world and the lover of knowledge.

Whenever they rebuild an old building, they must first of all destroy the old one.

Your radiance shines in every atom of creation yet our petty desires keep it hidden.

Everything about yesterday has gone with yesterday. Today, it is needed to say new things.

Why are you knocking at every door? Go, knock at the door of your own heart.

RUMI QUOTES ABOUT LOVE, MARRIAGE, PASSION

Lovers don't finally meet somewhere. They're in each other all along.

May these vows and this marriage be blessed. You have within you more love than you could ever understand.

When you seek love with all your heart you shall find its echo in the universe.

If you want to win hearts, sow the seeds of Love. If you want heaven, stop scattering thorns on the road.

This is love: to fly toward a secret sky, to cause a hundred veils to fall each moment. First to let go of life. Finally, to take a step without feet.

The minute I heard my first love story I started looking for you, not knowing how blind that was. Lovers don't finally meet somewhere. They're in each other all along.

Goodbyes are only for those who love with their eyes. Because for those who love with heart and soul there is no such thing as separation.

When I am with you, we stay up all night. When you're not here, I can't go to sleep.

There is no salvation for the soul but to fall in love. Only lovers can escape out of these two worlds.

This is what love does and continues to do. It tastes like honey to adults and milk to children.

I once had a thousand desires. But in my one desire to know you all else melted away.

I have no companion but Love, no beginning, no end, no dawn. The soul calls from within me: 'You, ignorant of the way of Love, set me free.'

On the path of love we are neither masters nor the owners of our lives. We are only a brush in the hand of the master painter.

Whatever happens, just keep smiling and lose yourself in love.

This sky where we live is no place to lose your wings so love, love, love.

Why ever talk of miracles when you are destined to become infinite love.

When we practice loving kindness and compassion we are the first ones to profit.

I am yours. Don't give myself back to me.

If you love someone, you are always joined with them – in joy, in absence, in solitude, in strife.

Let your teacher be love itself.

This is a subtle truth. Whatever you love, you are.

There is a path from me to you that I am constantly looking for.

Let yourself be drawn by the stronger pull of that which you truly love.

Every moment is made glorious by the light of love.

Now I am sober and there's only the hangover and the memory of love.

RUMI QUOTES ABOUT LIFE, HAPPINESS, WORRYING, JOY

Travel brings power and love back into your life.

Why should I be weary when every cell of my body is bursting with life?

Tend to your vital heart, and all that you worry about will be solved.

Caught by our own thoughts, we worry about everything.

Do not worry if all the candles in the world flicker and die. We have the spark that starts the fire.

Come out of the circle of time and into the circle of love.

This being human is a guest house. Every morning is a new arrival. A joy, a depression, a meanness, some momentary awareness comes as an unexpected visitor... Welcome and entertain them all. Treat each guest honorably. The dark thought, the shame, the malice, meet them at the door laughing, and invite them in. Be grateful for whoever comes, because each has been sent as a guide from beyond.

When I run after what I think I want, my days are a furnace of distress and anxiety; If I sit in my own place of patience, what I need flows to me, and without any pain. From this I understand that what I want also wants me, is looking for me and attracting me. There is a great secret in this for anyone who can grasp it.

There is a life in you, search that life, search the secret jewel in the mountain of your body.

Observe the wonders as they occur around you. Don't claim them. Feel the artistry moving through and be silent. Don't grieve. Anything you lose comes round in another form.

Oh soul, you worry too much. You have seen your own strength. You have seen your own beauty. You have seen your golden wings. Of anything less, why do you worry? You are in truth the soul, of the soul, of the soul.

My head is bursting with the joy of the unknown. My heart is expanding a thousand fold.

Why should I be unhappy? Every parcel of my being is in full bloom.

Oh! Joy for he who has escaped from this world of perfumes and color! For beyond these colors and these perfumes, these are other colors in the heart and the soul.

Be grateful for your life, every detail of it, and your face will come to shine like a sun, and everyone who sees it will be made glad and peaceful.

The illuminated life can happen now, in the moments left. Die to your ego, and become a true human being.

Travelers, it is late. Life's sun is going to set. During these brief days that you have strength, be quick and spare no effort of your wings.

If destiny comes to help you, love will come to meet you. A life without love isn't a life.

When you feel a peaceful joy, that's when you are near truth.
Joy lives concealed in grief.

Don't make yourself miserable with what is to come or not to come.

I learned that every mortal will taste death. But only some will taste life.

With life as short as a half-taken breath, don't plant anything but love.

Be kind and honest, and harmful poisons will turn sweet inside you.

If you want money more than anything, you'll be bought and sold your whole life.

Listen to the unstruck sounds, and what sifts through that music.

QUOTES BY RUMI ON FRIENDSHIP

Your heart and my heart are very, very old friends.

My heart, sit only with those who know and
understand you.

There is nothing I want but your presence. In
friendship, time dissolves.

Let's rise above this animalistic behavior and be
kind to one another.

Be a helpful friend, and you will become a green
tree with always new fruit, always deeper journeys
into love.

Stay with friends who support you in these. Talk
with them about sacred texts, and how you are

doing, and how they are doing, and keep your practices together.

Always search for your innermost nature in those you are with, as rose oil imbibes from roses.

My friend, the sufi is the friend of the present moment. To say tomorrow is not our way.

A warm, rainy day-this is how it feels when friends get together. Friend refreshes friend then, as flowers do each others, in a spring rain.

Words are a pretext. It is the inner bond that draws one person to another, not words.

Friendship of the wise is good; a wise enemy is better than a foolish friend.

If you are looking for a friend who is faultless, you will be friendless.

Why struggle to open a door between us when the whole wall is an illusion?

Friend, our closeness is this: anywhere you put your foot, feel me in the firmness under you.

Be with those who help your being.

QUOTES BY RUMI ON SADNESS, HEALING, PAIN, DEATH, LOSS, GRIEF

Whenever sorrow comes, be kind to it. For God has placed a pearl in sorrow's hand.

What hurts you, blesses you. Darkness is your candle.

Your depression is connected to your insolence and refusal to praise.

Don't grieve. Anything you lose comes round in another form.

This place is a dream. Only a sleeper considers it real. Then death comes like dawn, and you wake up laughing at what you thought was your grief.

Don't dismiss the heart, even if it's filled with sorrow. God's treasures are buried in broken hearts.

Don't be sad! Because God sends hope in the most desperate moments. Don't forget, the heaviest rain comes out of the darkest clouds.

Whatever sorrow shakes from your heart, far better things will take their place.

Sorrow prepares you for joy. It violently sweeps everything out of your house, so that new joy can find space to enter. It shakes the yellow leaves from the bough of your heart, so that fresh, green leaves can grow in their place.

Sorrow… It pulls up the rotten roots, so that new roots hidden beneath have room to grow. Whatever sorrow shakes from your heart, far better things will take their place.

Join the community of saints and know the delight of your own soul. Enter the ruins of your heart and learn the meaning of humility.

Grief can be the garden of compassion. If you keep your heart open through everything, your pain can become your greatest ally in your life's search for love and wisdom.

The wound is the place where the light enters you.

Whoever finds love beneath hurt and grief disappears into emptiness with a thousand new disguises.

But listen to me. For one moment quit being sad. Hear blessings dropping their blossoms around you.

Everyone is overridden by thoughts; that's why they have so much heartache and sorrow.

One of the marvels of the world: The sight of a soul sitting in prison with the key in its hand.

Don't turn away. Keep your gaze on the bandaged place. That's where the light enters you.

Don't get lost in your pain, know that one day your pain will become your cure.

Be patient where you sit in the dark. The dawn is coming.

Where there is ruin, there is hope for a treasure.

Suffering is a gift; in its hidden mercy.

Greed makes man blind and foolish, and makes him an easy prey for death.

QUOTES BY RUMI ON PEACE, INNER PEACE, GRATITUDE, SILENCE

Do you pay regular visits to yourself? Start now.

Prayer clears the mist and brings back peace to the soul.

Make peace with the universe. Take joy in it.

Do good to the people for the sake of God or for the peace of your own soul that you may always see what is pure and save your heart from the darkness of hate.

If you could get rid of yourself just once, the secret of secrets would open to you. The face of the unknown, hidden beyond the universe would appear on the mirror of your perception.

Make peace with the universe. Take joy in it. It will turn to gold. Resurrection will be now. Every moment, a new beauty.

Our greatest strength lies in the gentleness and tenderness of our heart.
A little while alone in your room will prove more valuable than anything else that could ever be given you.

This silence, this moment, every moment, if it's genuinely inside you, brings what you need. There's nothing to believe. Only when I stopped believing in myself did I come into this beauty. Sit quietly, and listen for a voice that will say, 'Be more silent.' Die and be quiet.

Quietness is the surest sign that you've died. Your old life was a frantic running from silence. Move outside the tangle of fear-thinking. Live in silence.

A wealth you cannot imagine flows through you. Do not consider what strangers say. Be secluded in your secret heart-house, that bowl of silence.

Stop, open up, surrender the beloved blind silence. Stay there until you see you're looking at the light with infinite eyes.

When all your desires are distilled; You will cast just two votes – to love more, and be happy.

Whatever happens to you, don't fall in despair. Even if all the doors are closed, a secret path will be there for you that no one knows. You can't see it yet but so many paradises are at the end of this path…Be grateful! It is easy to thank after obtaining what you want, thank before having what you want.

My dear heart, never think you are better than others. Listen to their sorrows with compassion. If you want peace, don't harbor bad thoughts, do not gossip and don't teach what you do not know.

Everything is emptiness. Everything else, accidental. Emptiness brings peace to your loving. Everything else, disease. In this world of trickery, emptiness is what your soul wants.

There is one way of breathing that is shameful and constricted. Then, there's another way: a breath of love that takes you all the way to infinity.

That which is false troubles the heart, but truth brings joyous tranquility.

Today, let us swim wildly, joyously in gratitude.

Wear gratitude like a cloak and it will feed every corner of your life.

Thankfulness brings you to the place where the beloved lives.

QUOTES BY RUMI ON BEAUTY, UNIVERSE

Do not feel lonely, the entire universe is inside you.

Everything in the universe is within you. Ask all from yourself.

The only lasting beauty is the beauty of the heart.

Shine like the whole universe is yours.
Everything that is made beautiful and fair and lovely is made for the eye of one who sees.

On a day when the wind is perfect, the sail just needs to open and the world is full of beauty. Today is such a day.

The very center of your heart is where life begins.
The most beautiful place on earth.

The sky will bow down to your beauty, if you do.

You have forgotten the One who doesn't care about
ownership, who doesn't try to turn a profit from
every human exchange.

The universe and the light of the stars come
through me.

The beauty you see in me is a reflection of you.

RUMI QUOTES ON NATURE, OCEAN, WATER, LIGHT, THE SUN, MOON

Your light is more magnificent than sunrise or sunset.

The breeze at dawn has secrets to tell you. Don't go back to sleep.

What hurts the soul? To live without tasting the water of its own essence.

We can't help being thirsty, moving toward the voice of water.

When water gets caught in habitual whirlpools, dig a way out through the bottom of the ocean.

There is a moon inside every human being. Learn to be companions with it.

Who could be so lucky? Who comes to a lake for water and sees the reflection of moon.

Be like the sun for grace and mercy. Be like the night to cover others' faults. Be like running water for generosity. Be like death for rage and anger. Be like the Earth for modesty. Appear as you are. Be as you appear.

Daylight, full of small dancing particles and the one great turning, our souls are dancing with you, without feet, they dance. Can you see them when I whisper in your ear?

You have no need to travel anywhere – journey within yourself. Enter a mine of rubies and bathe in the splendor of your own light.

If you wish to shine like day, burn up the night of self-existence. Dissolve in the Being who is everything.

Your heart is the size of an ocean. Go find yourself in its hidden depths.

Let the waters settle and you will see the moon and the stars mirrored in your own being.

Wherever water flows, life flourishes: wherever tears fall, divine mercy is shown.

How do I know who I am or where I am? How could a single wave locate itself in an ocean.

I have found the heart and will never leave this house of light.

Don't you know yet? It is your Light that lights the worlds.

Your task? To work with all the passion of your being to acquire an inner light.

Truth lifts the heart, like water refreshes thirst.

Love is the water of life, jump into this water.

Listen to the sound of waves within you.

RUMI QUOTES ON DANCE

We rarely hear the inward music, but we're all
dancing to it nevertheless.

Whosoever knoweth the power of the dance,
dwelleth in God.

Dancing is when you rise above both worlds,
tearing your heart to pieces and giving up your soul.

Without love, all worship is a burden, all dancing is
a chore, all music is mere noise.

In your light I learn how to love. In your beauty, how
to make poems. You dance inside my chest where

no-one sees you, but sometimes I do, and that sight becomes this art.

Dance, when you're broken open. Dance, if you've torn the bandage off. Dance in the middle of the fighting. Dance in your blood. Dance when you're perfectly free.

A divine dance appears in the soul and the body at the time of peace and union. Anyone can learn the dance, just listen to the music.

Dancing is not just getting up painlessly, like a leaf blown on the wind; dancing is when you tear your heart out and rise out of your body to hang suspended between the worlds.

Be kind to yourself, dear – to our innocent follies. Forget any sounds or touch you knew that did not help you dance. You will come to see that all evolves us.

In order to understand the dance one must be still. And in order to truly understand stillness one must dance.

Dance where you can break yourself up to pieces and totally abandon your worldly passions.

Dance, and make joyous the love around you. Dance, and your veils which hide the Light shall swirl in a heap at your feet.

We came whirling out of nothingness, scattering stars like dust… The stars made a circle, and in the middle, we dance.

I am a drunkard from another kind of tavern. I dance to a silent tune. I am the symphony of stars.

There are many ways to the Divine. I have chosen the ways of song, dance, and laughter.

RUMI QUOTES ON HOPE, STRENGTH, TRUST, FEAR, CHANGE

There are a thousand ways to kneel and kiss the ground; there are a thousand ways to go home again.

The Prophets accept all agony and trust it. For the water has never feared the fire.

Put your thoughts to sleep, do not let them cast a shadow over the moon of your heart. Let go of thinking.

It is certain that an atom of goodness on the path of faith is never lost.

On what is fear: Non-acceptance of uncertainty. If we accept that uncertainty, it becomes an adventure!

When you go through a hard period, when everything seems to oppose you, when you feel you cannot even bear one more minute, never give up! Because it is the time and place that the course will divert!

Those who don't feel this love pulling them like a river, those who don't drink dawn like a cup of springwater or take in sunset like a supper, those who don't want to change, let them sleep.

Always remember you are braver than you believe, stronger than you seem, smarter than you think and twice as beautiful as you'd ever imagined.

Why are you so enchanted by this world, when a mine of gold lies within you?

You were born with potential. You were born with goodness and trust. You were born with ideals and dreams. You were born with greatness. You were born with wings.

You are not meant for crawling, so don't. You have wings. Learn to use them and fly.

If something makes you happy in this world, you should think of what will happen to you if that thing were taken away.

If reason dominates in man, he rises higher than angels. If lust overpowers man, he descends lower than the beast.

Move, but don't move the way fear makes you move.

The garden of the world has no limits except in your mind

Looking up gives light, although at first it makes you dizzy.

RUMI SAYINGS ON GOD, SPIRITUALITY, RELIGION

I searched for God and found only myself. I searched for myself and found only God.

Silence is the language of God, all else is poor translation.

Each moment contains a hundred messages from God.

Touched. How did you get here? Close your eyes... and surrender!

Would you become a pilgrim on the road of love?
The first condition is that you make yourself humble
as dust and ashes.

Love is the water of life. Everything other than love
for the most beautiful God is agony of the spirit,
though it be sugar-eating. What is agony of the
spirit? To advance toward death without seizing
hold of the water of life.

If in thirst you drink water from a cup, you see God
in it. Those who are not in love with God will see
only their own faces in it.

To become spiritual, you must die to self, and come
alive in the Lord. Only then will the mysteries of
God fall from your lips. To die to self through self-
discipline causes suffering but brings you
everlasting life.

There is a loneliness more precious than life. There is a freedom more precious than the world. Infinitely more precious than life and the world is that moment when one is alone with God.

Knock, and He'll open the door. Vanish, and He'll make you shine like the sun. Fall, and He'll raise you to the heavens. Become nothing, and He'll turn you into everything.

Sit quietly and listen for a voice that will say, "Be more silent." As that happens, your soul starts to revive.

Till man destroys "self" he is no true friend of God.

Now be silent. Let the One who creates the words speak. He made the door. He made the lock. He also made the key.

Ways of worshipping are not to be ranked as better or worse than one another… It's all praise, and it's all right.

We are all the same… all the same… longing to find our way back… back to the One… back to the only One!

Why, when God's world is so big, did you fall asleep in a prison, of all places?

God turns you from one feeling to another and teaches by means of opposites so that you will have two wings to fly, not one

Stay in the spiritual fire. Let it cook you.

All religions. All this singing. One song. Peace be with you.

I am in the House of Mercy, and my heart is a place of prayer.

RUMI POEMS ABOUT LOVE, LIFE

Poem #1
Love came and became like blood in my body.
It rushed through my veins and encircled my heart.

Poem #2
I will be waiting here…
For your silence to break,
for your soul to shake,
for your love to wake.

Poem #3
I was dead, then alive.
Weeping, then laughing.
The power of love came into me,
and I became fierce like a lion,
then tender like the evening star.

Poem #4

I choose to love you in silence, for in silence I find
no rejection.
I choose to love you in loneliness, for in loneliness
no one owns you but me.
I choose to adore you from a distance. For distance
will shield me from pain.
I choose to kiss you in the wind, for the wind is
gentler than my lips.
I choose to hold you in my dreams, for me in
dreams, you have no ends.

Poem #5

I have lived on the lip of insanity,
wanting to know reasons,
knocking on a door.
It opens.
I've been knocking from the inside.

Poem #6

I've been looking for a long, long time,
for this thing called love,
I've ridden comets across the sky,
and I've looked below and above.
Then one day I looked inside myself,
and this is what I found,
a golden sun residing there,
beaming forth God's light and sound.

Poem #7

I am so close, I may look distant.
So completely mixed with you, I may look separate.
So out in the open, I appear hidden.
So silent, because I am constantly talking with you.

Poem #8

I was a tiny bug.
Now a mountain.
I was left behind.
Now honored at the head.
You healed my wounded hunger and anger,
and made me a poet who sings about joy.

Poem #9
Sometimes in order to help He makes us cry.
Happy the eye that sheds tears for His sake.
Fortunate the heart that burns for His sake.
Laughter always follow tears.
Blessed are those who understand.
Life blossoms wherever water flows.
Where tears are shed divine mercy is shown

Poem #10
Doing as others told me, I was blind.
Coming when others called me, I was lost.
Then I left everyone, myself as well.
Then I found everyone, myself as well.

Poem #11
This is how it always is when I finish a poem.
A great silence overcomes me
and I wonder why I ever thought to use language.

Made in United States
North Haven, CT
22 September 2022

24373418R00050